Original title:
The Mango Blossom

Copyright © 2025 Creative Arts Management OÜ
All rights reserved.

Author: Ronan Whitfield
ISBN HARDBACK: 978-1-80586-443-1
ISBN PAPERBACK: 978-1-80586-915-3

Cradle of Summer's Light

In the sun's warm embrace, they sway,
Laughing leaves dance in disarray.
Honeybees buzz with fuzzy charm,
Won't they just cause a slight alarm?

Gentle whispers of the heat,
Tickling toes and friendly feet.
A playful breeze brings giggles near,
As petals blush—a comedy here!

Glistening Petals by Twilight

As the day slips into night,
Glowing petals shine so bright.
Bouncing light upon the ground,
A show of colors all around!

Fireflies weave between the blooms,
Thinking they're in fancy costumes.
They twirl and spin in silly flight,
A dance party in fading light!

Secrets of the Tropical Breeze

Whispers carried through the trees,
Mischief shared by the warmest breeze.
It tickles cheeks and tousles hair,
Secret laughter fills the air.

The wind plays tricks, how it sways,
Inviting smiles on sunny days.
Like a prankster, it won't relent,
Wishing for fun to be well-spent!

Symphony of Vibrant Colors

A riot of hues in the sun's glow,
Like a painter's palette, stealing the show.
Each shade sings a tune so bright,
Crafting a concert of pure delight.

From citrus yellows to berry reds,
The audience chuckles, lifting their heads.
Nature's laughter, a melody rare,
In this vibrant clash, joy fills the air!

The Serenade of Color

In a sea of vibrant cheer,
A flower tickles a buzzing bee.
"Hey there, friend, come lend an ear,
I've got jokes, just wait and see!"

Petals dance in swaying breeze,
Whispers shared with rustling leaves.
A fruit nearby laughs with ease,
"I'm ripe for fun, so just believe!"

Laughter in the Orchard

In the grove where colors shine,
Orchard tales bring giggles quick.
A silly sprite made of vine,
Juggles fruits with a mighty kick!

Squirrels chuckle atop the trees,
As they spy antics from below.
"Guard these treasures if you please!"
The laughter spreads like seeds in tow.

Unfurling Underneath the Sky

With a stretch and a joyful yawn,
A bloom declares, "Here comes the fun!"
Twinkling petals wink at dawn,
Sunlight dances, laughter spun!

Bumbling bees in a merry race,
Hover near with cheeky grins.
"Join our buzz, and quicken pace!"
The joy of spring is where it begins.

Hues of Heartfelt Sunshine

Bright colors play hide and seek,
In a patch where giggles grow.
Bouncing fruits, oh what a peek!
"Catch us if you can!" they crow.

From the laughter, seeds are sown,
Sprouting joy amongst the vines.
In a funny twist, they've grown,
To tickle hearts with fruity signs.

Dance of the Blossoming Trees

In a garden where flowers conspire,
The branches sway with laughter, higher.
Petals twirl in a silly ballet,
As bees join in and hum all day.

Each flower winks, a cheeky tease,
Swinging in the wind with breezy ease.
Oh, the joy of springtime's prance,
Nature throws a wild, carefree dance.

Midnight's Call to Daylight

At midnight, petals dream and snore,
Roused by sunbeams at their door.
A yawning bloom, unable to fight,
Sips the morning, in pure delight.

With coffee beans or honeydew,
They giggle bright and blushing too.
The sun says, 'Hey, rise and shine!'
While flowers stretch, feeling just fine!

Whispering Colors of Spring

Colors jive in a cheerful scheme,
Red whispers secrets to bright green dreams.
Yellow chortles, 'I'm the sun's best friend!'
While blue and pink around the bend.

Splashing hues in a playful race,
Each hue tries to take up space.
But in the end, they laugh and sway,
Together painting a perfect day!

Pollen's Poetry

Pollen drifts like tiny bits of cheer,
Tickling noses, spreading good vibes here.
It sneezes lighthearted in the breeze,
Making flowers giggle, if you please!

'Bless you!' cries the playful breeze,
As pollen dances, crossing trees.
In this garden of rhyme and jest,
Nature's humor is surely the best!

Tropic Hues Unveiled

In the sun, a fruit with flair,
Dancing on trees, no time to spare.
With petals bright, they giggle a tune,
While bees all buzz, in a wild cartoon.

A hat of green, the leaves play coy,
Swaying to winds, like a playful toy.
Fruits beneath, they tease and shout,
"Pick me first! Come on, don't pout!"

A touch of sweet, a splash of zest,
In candy dreams, they jest the best.
When the rain falls, they jump and splash,
Leaving puddles—oh, what a bash!

With every fruit, a smile's cast,
Joyful laughter, a spell unsurpassed.
Under the sun, they play all day,
In nature's circus, they dance and sway.

Enchanted Seasons of Delight

In a garden where giggles grow,
Flowers wear crowns, and breezes flow.
With a wink and a sway, in bright arrays,
They charm the sun, in comical plays.

Whispers of sweetness fill the air,
As butterflies dance, without a care.
Each blossom thinks it's quite the star,
While neighbors say, "You're bizarre!"

A breeze tickles, petals take flight,
Spinning around in pure delight.
With a little hop, they paint the sky,
Joking with clouds as they pass by.

In this realm of laughter divine,
Every burst of color, a slapstick line.
Where joy is king and fun's the game,
Each petal giggles, forgets its name!

Blossoms in Lush Abundance

In the orchard, giggles soar,
A fruit parade, who could ask for more?
Bees wearing hats, buzzing in tune,
While squirrels juggle nuts, under the moon.

Petals rain down like confetti bright,
As I slip on a bloom, oh, what a sight!
The gardener's spade, a sword in jest,
Fighting weeds dressed as guests at a fest.

Colorful Echoes of Youth

Children skip, their laughter flies,
While color drops draw a thousand sighs.
A parrot squawks jokes, on a playful spree,
Telling tales as wild as a fruit tree's glee.

Each petal a ticket for a fun ride,
As butterflies flaunt, wings open wide.
Little hearts race, feet pitter-pat,
Chasing shadows and laughter, oh, imagine that!

Dance of Fluttering Wings

A dance-off between blooms and buzzing flies,
Tripping on petals, oh, what a surprise!
One little critter, with moves so strange,
Stepped on a daisy, made it rearrange.

Caterpillars twist like rubbery bands,
In the grand ballroom of sunny lands.
While ladybugs waltz with such grand flair,
Catching sunbeams in their delicate snare.

Petal Dreams on the Breeze

A playful wind whispers silly tunes,
Disguising itself as silly balloons.
Flying through fields, it pranks and twirls,
Tickling the petals, giving laughs and swirls.

Clouds chuckle softly, puffed and white,
Watching flower-fights, oh what a sight!
In this carnival of color and cheer,
Every moment is silly, that much is clear!

Lush Gardens of Youth

In vibrant greens, we chase the sun,
A fruit so sweet, it's never done.
Laughter spills like juice from trees,
Underneath the buzzing bees.

We'd climb the branches, oh what a sight,
Swinging like monkeys, pure delight.
Green thumbs and mischief in the air,
Now that's a childhood affair!

A Dance of Pollinators

Bees and butterflies swirl around,
In the orchard where joy is found.
They flap and zoom, a playful crew,
Dressed in colors, bright and new.

With each bloom, they spin and twirl,
Nature's dancers in a whirl.
A flower's wink, a bug's loud cheer,
It's a party, come join, my dear!

Citrus Kisses on Gentle Breezes

A sunlit day with citrus scents,
Breezes blow, the moment's tense.
We chase the fruit, we reach, we run,
A tangerine? What a fun!

It rolls away, oh what a tease,
The laughter echoes in the trees.
With sticky fingers, we share the prize,
Underneath those sunny skies!

Secrets of a Tropical Grove

In shadows deep, secrets collide,
A playful fruit, with mischievous pride.
Whispers of flavor, bold and good,
Hidden treasures in the wood.

We sneak a bite, giggles erupt,
Juicy dribbles and silly hiccup.
The grove's a stage for jests and cheer,
Where nature's laughter is crystal clear!

Harmony Amongst Leaves

In a dance of green, they sway,
Tiny buds with much to say.
Wobbling branches, a jolly sight,
Singing tunes in morning light.

Petals giggle in a breeze,
Racing sunlight with such ease.
Dewdrops laugh, they jump and play,
Sharing secrets of the day.

Fragrance of Quiet Days

A whiff of joy floats by,
Eager bees begin to fly.
Whispers tickle, bees take flight,
On this sweet and sunny night.

Butterflies wear silly hats,
Dancing round like playful cats.
Nature's humor all around,
In this fragrant, silly ground.

Radiating Joy in Bloom

A burst of colors bright and bold,
Dancing stories, laughter told.
Blossoms prance with cheeky cheer,
Making every day feel dear.

Sunshine winks from leafy nooks,
While ladybugs read fun books.
Petals tickle as they fall,
Nature's jest, a joyful call.

A Canvas of Natural Delight

With a brush of bright green hue,
Squirrels paint the sky so blue.
Chirping birds join in the fun,
Every splash a joy to run.

A canvas stretched where laughter grows,
Colorful tales the flower knows.
Joyful whims, a playful art,
Nature's canvas warms the heart.

Essence of Warmth

A tree stands tall, a sight to behold,
With flowers so sweet, more precious than gold.
Bees buzz around, doing their dance,
While squirrels around, in chaos, prance.

A pop of yellow, a splash of cheer,
I giggle at friends competing for beer.
The sun laughs bright, planting silly dreams,
As pollen floats on laughter's beams.

Embracing Life's Tender Moments

In the garden's glow, there's mischief afoot,
Lemons make faces, while oranges just hoot.
Flowers giggle in a chorus of hues,
Encouraging laughter, though none have shoes.

A tiny worm wears a crown made of leaf,
He claims he's the king, oh what a belief!
Butterflies waltz with a glamorous flair,
While ants plan a feast, with maniacal stare.

Flourish in Sun's Embrace

Under bright rays, the garden did grow,
With quirks and laughter, stealing the show.
Dandelions giggle when they offer a wish,
While cabbage whispers, 'Come, take a swish!'

Sunshine bathes all in colorful glee,
A jester of nature, oh how it will be!
The shadows dance lightly, avoiding the light,
As crickets play tunes throughout the night.

A Tapestry of Beauty

Colors collide in a riotous play,
With bees hoarding laughter, storing it away.
Tiny seed pockets of joy all around,
As the breeze tells secrets where smiles abound.

A caricature blooms, wild and fun,
With giggles and chuckles, the day's just begun.
Fruits compete for who's prettiest here,
Sprouting a contest, let's all give a cheer!

Adorned in Nature's Bounty

In the garden, a joke plays wide,
Petals wear crowns, with pride, they glide.
Bees buzzing laugh, they're quite the bees,
Tickling blossoms with their buzzing tease.

Colors clash like a paint fight spree,
Butterfly giggles, flutters carefree.
Swaying like dancers on a sunny stage,
Nature's folly fills every page.

Tender Petals in the Breeze

In a breeze, petals take a spin,
They toss and twirl, all grins and din.
Stumbling over each other in flight,
As if they're playing tag, all delight.

A breeze whispers secrets, a ticklish tease,
Leave it to petals, they do as they please.
Every sway is a chance for a laugh,
Nature's mimes doing their little half.

Blooming in Quietude

In silent bloom, a giggle grows,
Petals make quiet needs for funny shows.
Gardener's struggle with unruly weeds,
Each slip and trip, the garden leads.

With a chuckle, they sprout and sway,
As if they've plotted, 'Let's laugh today!'
In this stillness, a joy takes flight,
Blooming giggles in soft morning light.

Oasis of Joy

A quirky oasis, where laughter flows,
Blossoms tease the sun, and everyone knows.
The lizards sunbathe, wearing shades, so cool,
While the flowers gossip, skirting the rule.

The water rejoices, it splashes with glee,
As frogs croak jokes that make bees agree.
In this lively patch, the world feels bright,
Where even the shadows dance in delight.

Tranquil Moments in Bloom

In a garden lush and bright,
Flowers dance in sheer delight,
Bees wear shades, a buzzing crew,
Stealing nectar, oh so blue!

Petals sway with giggles light,
Tickling bees in joyful flight,
Nature's laughter fills the air,
As butterflies play peek-a-boo there!

Squirrels chase their tails in glee,
Climbing branches like a spree,
Each blossom shares a wink and grin,
In this world, we all fit in!

Nature's jokes we love to share,
With every breeze, there's fun to spare,
Laughter blooms where hearts convene,
In the days of greenest sheen!

The Beauty of Gentle Caresses

Softly brushing 'gainst the leaves,
A tickling touch that never grieves,
The sun peeks through with golden rays,
Making laughter fill our days.

Winds whisper secrets, sweet and silly,
Rustling blooms, oh what a filly!
Petals blush in softest hues,
Playing dress-up in playful dues!

Dancing shadows on the ground,
Where whimsical tales abound,
Nature's brush paints with a flair,
In the joy that fills the air!

Every gust a giggle strong,
Nature's tune, a cheeky song,
With each petal's soft embrace,
Life unfolds with laughter's grace!

Stories Written in Petals

Once a bud with dreams so grand,
Wrote sweet tales upon the sand,
Each petal penned a line or two,
About sunlit skies and morning dew.

Beetles taking turns to read,
Rascally ants, they cheer and lead,
A narrative of joy and fun,
As the playful stories run!

A jester bloom with stripes so bold,
Spinning yarns that never get old,
With laughter heard in every breeze,
Each flower shares a tale with ease!

So here beneath the sky so blue,
Petals whisper secrets true,
In this vibrant garden glade,
Where stories bloom and never fade!

Morning's Dew-kissed Embrace

The sun peeks up, a cheeky grin,
As dew drops dance on every skin,
Tiny fairies skip with glee,
Playing tag around the tree.

Each blade of grass wears sparkly crowns,
As morning yawns, and nods around,
Bees and bugs in joyful haste,
Join the fun, no time to waste!

A sleepy flower starts to crack,
Revealing colors, bright and whack,
In the warmth, they stretch and pose,
While the cheeky sun gently glows!

Awakened buds embrace the day,
Where fun and laughter sweetly play,
Beneath the sky, with hearts so free,
Morning's joy, a playful spree!

Vibrant Choir of Petals

In the garden, petals dance,
Each twirl creates a glance.
The bees hum their sweet delight,
While squirrels crash the show, oh what a sight!

Colors clash in a lively spree,
A floral band, a jolly jubilee.
With butterflies as the VIPs,
They sip nectar, giggling in the breeze.

A lizard struts with quite the flair,
Nature's stage, we stop and stare.
Frogs croak out a silly tune,
While blooms on trees just shake and swoon.

Petal parties, who needs a wall?
The garden's got the funniest call.
Under sun's laughter, we all unite,
With vibrant petals shining bright!

Essence of Summer's Lullaby

Underneath the warming rays,
Nature sings in quirky ways.
A breeze that tickles, a sun so bold,
Bringing tales of warmth, retold.

Bees wear hats, oh what a sight,
They dance with flowers, oh so light.
Crickets chirp with gusto and cheer,
Join the chorus, the insects are here!

A butterfly pranks the busy ant,
"Catch me, catch me!"—the ants' big chant.
Laughter ripples through the green,
In the silliness, all is seen.

As day winks and night arrives,
The giggles linger, the humor thrives.
In this sonnet of sunny spree,
A lullaby just tickles me!

Treasure of the Orchard

Orchard treasures, sweet and rare,
With fruits that dangle, quite the affair.
Squirrels plot in their nutty plans,
While birds practice their most funny scans.

With every bob and dip and swoop,
The harvest sings a playful loop.
Some fruits wobble, others sigh,
In this orchard, oh my, oh my!

The laughter ripens on each limb,
As wind plays a funny whim.
Pigeons coo like they're on stage,
In this vibrant, fruity page.

With every crunch, a giggle spills,
Juicy bites give all the thrills.
What a treasure, pure delight,
In the orchard's funny light!

Sun-kissed Resilience

Beneath the sun's warm, golden gaze,
Life bounces back through funny ways.
Forget the rain, it's all in jest,
Survival in style, we're truly blessed.

A plant stretching with a goofy grin,
Finding sunlight through thick and thin.
Insects giggle, giving their cheer,
While flowers dance, no room for fear.

With roots that twist and leave their mark,
Each obstacle's a whimsical lark.
Though storms may bring a little frown,
The sun-kissed spirit won't back down!

Through ups and downs, we'll find our beat,
In nature's rhythm, we'll skip our feet.
So here's to laughter, bright and wide,
With resilience and fun as our guide!

Secrets in the Garden

In the garden, secrets hide,
Where odd-shaped fruits roll and slide.
A squirrel steals a lime with glee,
Chasing butterflies like it's free.

The chatty bees tell silly tales,
Of flower races and silly snails.
While rabbits giggle, sharing dreams,
Of all the snacks and berry creams.

The soil trembles, plants do dance,
As worms throw parties at first glance.
A cucumber in a hat smiles wide,
Declares it's time for joy and pride.

Oh, the whispers of veggie cheer,
In the garden, laughter's near.
Every vine and leaf agrees,
To spread a laugh upon the breeze.

Jewel of the Tropics

In the tropics where sunshine beams,
Jellybeans fall from leafy seams.
A parrot wears a vibrant tie,
As mangoes giggle from the sky.

An iguana plays a quirky tune,
Dancing wildly beneath the moon.
While coconuts roll like bowling balls,
Knocking down the fidgeting walls.

A pineapple throws a big fiesta,
With fruit punch madness, it's the best, yeah!
Mango candies fly around,
As laughter and smiles abound.

In the sun's bright, balmy rays,
Nature's humor brings sunny days.
Gather 'round, let's toast the cheer,
For every fruity friend that's near.

Vibrance in the Shade

Underneath the leafy cover,
A breeze brings stories; we discover.
Kittens chase shadows with delight,
As light dances, making things bright.

A wise old tortoise shares a joke,
About a fruit that learned to poke!
With giggles scattering like confetti,
The day turns lively, oh so zesty!

Banana boats go sailing by,
With laughter echoing in the sky.
Each tomfoolery, a sight to behold,
As stories spin and joy unfolds.

In this vibrant shade so lush,
Where each voice joins in the rush,
Nature's humor plays its part,
Crafting smiles straight from the heart.

Echoes of Summer Dreams

In the summer, dreams take flight,
As frolicking fruits bring pure delight.
A watermelon sings a summer tune,
While dancing petals twirl under the moon.

Lemons throw a zesty bash,
With slippery slides and quite the crash!
Mangoes wearing shades of gold,
Laugh at stories that are retold.

The sun beams down, and laughter swells,
As buzzing bees share all their spells.
Fruit friends gather, jump, and sway,
In a raucous dance that lasts all day.

Echoes of giggles fill the air,
As summer dreams spin without a care.
In this garden of fruits, we find,
The funny tales of nature entwined.

Symphony of Brightness

In a tree, a chatterbox sings,
With petals that twirl and dance like springs.
Bees buzz by, doing their quirky prance,
While squirrels try to join the floral romance.

A pitcher plant's got a sneaky plan,
To catch a clumsy fly—oh, what a jam!
Laughter echoes in the warm, soft air,
As butterflies twirl without a single care.

Each bloom wears a silly, sunny grin,
As the breeze tickles, let the fun begin.
But watch your head—here comes a playful seed,
Launching from the tree like a goofy steed!

A floral parade on this bright, green stage,
Where every bloom is a comical page.
Nature's circus, full of color and cheer,
Come join the ruckus, let's shout out "Oh dear!"

The Sun's Gentle Caress

Sunbeams dance, like friends at play,
Tickling leaves in a gentle ballet.
A playful breeze says, 'Catch me again!'
While rosy petals giggle, my dear friend.

One bloom teases another, 'Look at me! '
As they sway and sway, oh so carefree.
The sun rolls his eyes, 'Not this again!'
'Will you sit still? I'm trying to pretend!'

Down below, the worms wriggle and squirm,
Making mud pies with an earthworm's charm.
A beetle tosses a quick, funny glance,
And joins in on this glowing, goofy dance.

Together they bask in the comfort of light,
Celebrating the day, canceling the night.
Laughing at shadows that seem to appear,
Chasing away gloom, bringing in cheer.

Radiant Fragments of Joy

In the garden, laughter blooms bright,
As petals toss off their wearisome plight.
Every color splashes, a mischievous jest,
While the sun plays tag, doing its best!

A fluttering butterfly forgot how to fly,
With wings so wide, it's hard to comply.
It lands on a flower, thinking it's smart,
Then slips off the edge—oh, a comical start!

A hummingbird zooms like a tiny jet,
While the flowers raise their roots and fret.
They whisper secrets of nectar and fun,
While laughing at bees, thinking they've won.

The grass joins in with a tickle to toes,
While ants do the conga in silly rows.
Nature's amusement is a whimsical show,
With giggles and chuckles as bright blooms aglow.

Tender Touch of Warmth

The sunshine drizzles like honey on blooms,
While flowers play dress-up in nature's costumes.
With colors so vibrant, they laugh at the bees,
Who get dizzy with pollen—'Oh, please, oh please!'

A ladybug lounges, sipping on dew,
'What a day!' she sighs, with a wink and a chew.
While ants march in rhythm, a comedic parade,
Carrying crumbs, while they dance in the shade.

The wind crackles jokes as it rustles the trees,
Tickling branches and stirring the leaves.
A bumblebee buzzes with a silly grin,
Stumbling through petals, it wobbles and spins!

In this bright haven, where joy hits the ground,
Every giggle and whisper goes round and round.
Nature's delight, so playful and warm,
Gives life to the day, a delightful charm.

Pathways of Color and Light

In a garden where colors play,
Petals chase shadows all day.
Buzzing bees in a silly dance,
Sweet nectar draws them in a trance.

Laughter echoes through the breeze,
As flowers wink with playful tease.
A butterfly, dressed to impress,
Trips on petals in a mess!

Worms gossip under the ground,
About the silly sights they've found.
But in this charm of vibrant hue,
Even ants are known to coo!

Sunshine splashes colors bright,
A rainbow tugs the strings of light.
Every bloom is a witty jest,
In the garden, we're all guests!

Echoing Whispers of Spring

The flowers giggle, what a sight!
Blooming with joy, oh so bright!
A breeze comes in, a tickling tease,
Turning stiff leaves into a sneeze.

The sun peeks in with a cheeky grin,
While birds chirp out a wild din.
Chubby squirrels play hide and seek,
In bushes where they take a peek.

A frog croaks loud in froggy tunes,
Dancing under the laughing moons.
Every branch sways to the beat,
Of spring's orchestra, oh so sweet!

With each bloom, a jest unfolds,
Nature's joy in stories told.
Tickling petals, bursting cheer,
In this season, fun is near!

Garden of Enchantment

In this garden, plants like to play,
Welcome visitors with a sway.
Giggling daisies in a row,
Invite the bees to come and flow.

The roses gossip, they can't keep still,
About the thorns giving quite a thrill.
Hummingbirds zip with frantic grace,
Spilling nectar all over the place!

A patch of daisies sprout a laugh,
Rubbing petals on the giraffe!
Even the trees appear to smirk,
As the squirrels perform their work.

In this giggle fest of blooms so bold,
Every blossom has a story told.
Come join the laughter, don't be shy,
In this garden where fun can fly!

Timeless Beauty of Nature

Amidst the trees, a tall tale spins,
Where even the shadows wear silly grins.
Flowers pose for the windiest hair,
While sunlight flirts out everywhere.

A hapless rabbit trips on roots,
Chasing after some silly fruits.
Butterflies hold a fashion show,
With wings that shimmer in a glow.

Rustling leaves, they play tag and chase,
While petals blush in a bright embrace.
The world is giggling, can't you hear?
In nature's laughter, joy is near!

Here, time stands still in a chuckling way,
As the blooms come out to laugh and play.
Each sight, a stitch in the quilt of cheer,
Nature's humor, forever dear!

Sunlit Reverberations

In gardens where the sunlight plays,
A dance of petals, bright displays.
The buzzing bees, they hum and cheer,
As flowers giggle without any fear.

With colors bold and scents so sweet,
They fool the ants, who dance on feet.
A friendly breeze whispers a joke,
While blooms erupt in a laughter-stroke.

The sun would tip its hat, so proud,
As silly blooms attract a crowd.
They wink and nod in cheerful glee,
Oh, what a sight for all to see!

In this sunny riot of joy and fun,
Each blossom thinks it's number one.
As petals flap and fragrances tease,
Life is a party, bursting with ease.

The Language of Blossoms

Whispers in the garden chat,
What's new, my flowery hat?
They giggle in their pastel tones,
Making jokes with leafy groans.

One says, 'I'm feeling rather grand,
With all these bees, lend me a hand.'
Another chimes, 'They come and flee,
Perhaps they think they're here for tea!'

They trade funny tales of sunlight's plight,
And how to dance when the winds are light.
With every breeze, a joke unfolds,
As nature's comedy gently molds.

In petal hues so vibrant and bright,
They laugh till dusk, oh what a sight!
A secret language, all their own,
In blooms and laughter, joy has grown.

Heartbeats in Bloom

In this garden, the heartbeats thrum,
A chorus of laughter, oh so hum!
Each petal a pulse, a jolly beat,
As flowers nod to the rhythm sweet.

One petal winks with a flourished sway,
Says, 'Who knew blooms could have their play?'
Bouncing in the sunlight's warm embrace,
Spreading joy in this brightened space.

With a sway here and a twirl there,
They dance around without a care.
Their humor spreads, it's a fragrant spree,
A carnival of blossoms, wild and free.

Every flower in exuberant bloom,
Whispers joy that chases gloom.
Their giggles echo, a vibrant sound,
In this lively patch of life unbound.

A Fragrant Canvas

Nature paints with colors bold,
On canvas bright, stories unfold.
A playful bloom with a cheeky grin,
Shares silly secrets with the wind's spin.

Petals plot, and they conspire,
To spread good vibes that don't expire.
They challenge bees to a giggle race,
Who'll get the nectar, the fastest pace?

Amidst the leaves, a jest is born,
With every gust, new jokes are worn.
From morning light to twilight's glow,
In every laugh, sweet seeds they sow.

The garden's an artist, wild and free,
Creating joy for you and me.
In every fragrance, a story bugs,
Funny friendships sprout with hugs.

Dreamscapes of Abundant Life

In a garden of snacks, there's a sweet, juicy dream,
Where fruit rains from trees like a candy stream.
With laughter and giggles, the squirrels throw a feast,
And bees dance like jesters, quite the humorous beast.

The parakeets chime in with a raucous toast,
To a fruit salad party, where we're all the host.
Fuzzy peaches are jiving, a party on the run,
While sneaky little rabbits try to join in on the fun.

Flowers are wearing hats made of sunny delight,
While ants form a conga line, what a silly sight!
Moths flutter around like they can't find their chair,
As we munch on this banquet, with giggles to spare.

So let's raise our cups high to this fruity affair,
To the garden of laughter, and the joy in the air.
For in this wild dreamscape, let nothing be missed,
Join the feast of nature, in a laugh-worthy twist!

Sanctuary of Blossoms

In a realm where petals play hide and seek,
Butterflies giggle, while the tulips squeak.
A bumblebee buzzes, wearing shades so bright,
And the sunflowers gossip, what a comical sight.

Each blossom a character, with stories to share,
The daisies are dishing dirt, without a care.
A clumsy old caterpillar, falls into the pond,
While giggling lilacs whisper, 'He'll take quite a bond!'

The wind's playing tricks, with a flurry of fun,
Tugging at petals, making everyone run.
The violets are rolling, joyously in the grass,
While the roses blush crimson, when the daisies pass.

Here in this haven, where laughter does bloom,
Nothing's too serious, there's always room.
So come decked in giggles, to this flowered spree,
In the sanctuary of blossoms, come share the glee!

Beneath the Canopy of Hope

Under a leafy roof, where the fun never ends,
Squirrels recount tales while the branch gently bends.
Raindrops like marbles, spill stories of cheer,
As birds chirp in harmony; oh, what a year!

Mirth spills from the flowers, with petals like jokes,
The roots are all raucous, playing practical hoax.
A snail with a top hat, moves with pomp and style,
While shadows join in, for a dance with a smile.

The trees nod in rhythm, to the laughter below,
Casting their shade where the silly winds blow.
It's a riot of colors, a jubilant show,
Beneath this lush canopy, joy's sure to grow.

So let's gather together, each giggle a tie,
In this realm of delight, where spirits can fly.
For under the branches, where whimsy takes shape,
Hope lives and flourishes, in this fanciful grape!

Splendor in the Air

In the twilight of laughter, the fun takes a leap,
As fragrances mingle and joy starts to creep.
With humor intwined in the whispers of leaves,
Life's a side-splitting tale, that nobody deceives.

Breezes blow softly, like tickling a friend,
While dandelions chuckle, their wishes they send.
Clouds wear a smile, drifting playful and light,
In this splendorous moment, everything feels right.

The stars wink above, there's mischief in sight,
As fireflies blinky dance, in the warm summer night.
They're pulling a prank, with a glow and a flash,
While the moon giggles softly, as shadows all clash.

Let laughter be spread like confetti in air,
For this splendor of nature, we all gladly share.
In a world where the funny is cherished most dear,
Join the laughter and joy, for the magic is here!

Sweetness Entwined

In the garden a buzz, a bee on the chase,
Fumbling round flowers, what a silly race!
Sticky and sweet, he slips on a petal,
Dancing and twirling, oh what a medal!

A squirrel with a nibble, cheeky and spry,
Steals all the fruit, oh me, oh my!
With a wiggly tail and a giggle so grand,
He plants tiny seeds in the neighbors' garden stand!

Sunshine and laughter, the air's filled with cheer,
The little mischiefs bring joy, never fear!
Each bud is a joke, each twig a delight,
Nature's own comedy, such a funny sight!

So here's to the blooms, in their silly attire,
Life's sweetest moments, never will tire!
With a chuckle, we tend to the jests that they sow,
In the heart of our garden, where laughter will grow!

Garden's Gentle Symphony

In the morning light, the bugs all convene,
With crickets and beetles, what a raucous scene!
A grasshopper's solo, a frog's funny croak,
The blossoms all giggle, this tune is no joke!

The breeze starts to dance, twisting the leaves,
A twig snaps with a crack, oh how it deceives!
The petals all chuckle, as they rustle in glee,
While cacti look on, thinking, "Let's not be free!"

A snail took a tumble, it's stuck on a leaf,
"Excuse me, kind flower, I need relief!"
The roses just titter, "Oh, what a charm!"
As the snail waves its feelers, causing no harm.

In this jolly garden, where music is found,
Nature's sweet humor spins round and round!
With each little giggle and every soft sigh,
It's a concert of laughter beneath the blue sky!

Colorful Hues of Dawn

When the first light appears, bugs rise from their sleep,
Dewdrops are bouncing on blades, oh so deep!
A rainbow of colors, the petals all cheer,
Chasing away shadows, bringing in beer!

A parrot's loud squawk, wakes up the whole place,
As the flowers all roll, in a bright, happy race!
With colors so vivid, they giggle aloud,
Each hue telling tales, proud and unbowed!

The daisies are gossiping, sharing their news,
With pansies eavesdropping, in their fancy shoes!
It's quite the affair, a floral soirée,
Where laughter and fragrance twirl and ballet!

So here's to the colors, the giggles they bring,
In this vibrant morning where nature can sing!
With each playful burst, and each blush from the dawn,
The day starts with humor, and worries are gone!

Embrace of the Sunlit Grove

Underneath the tall trees, shadows play tricks,
While squirrels perform scrambles, all full of kicks!
They tumble and roll, branches creak with delight,
As the laughing leaves rustle, a whimsical sight!

A butterfly flutters, with a wink and a grin,
Whirling through petals, she's pulling them in!
With a jiggle and wiggle, she gives them a spin,
Creating a dance-party where all can begin!

The sun shines so bright, bathing all in its glow,
As critters gather 'round for the grand show!
Each flower's a player in this comedy troupe,
Sharing all secrets in nature's grand loop!

So waltz through the grove and let laughter resound,
In this playful haven, where joy can be found!
For every small chuckle and giggle we share,
Brings warmth to our hearts, and lightens the air!

In Praise of Nature's Palette

In a garden bright, colors collide,
A splash of yellow, a cheeky pride.
Bees buzz around, looking for snacks,
While butterflies dance, no time to relax.

Petals flaunt hues, a riotous show,
Our leafy friends join in, putting on a glow.
Nature's own fussy, delightful parade,
Even the grass tries to join the charade.

Sunshine giggles, the clouds play tag,
A painter's dream, with no room for drag.
With every hue, the world comes alive,
Who knew nature's palette would always jive?

Let's salute the blooms that tickle our sight,
Each day is a festival, pure delight!
In the garden of mischief, joy takes its chance,
And flowers wear smiles, ready to dance!

When Petals Meet the Wind

A breeze takes aim, it's time for some fun,
Petals fly high, oh what a run!
They skitter and scatter, like dancers in flight,
Trying to waltz, oh what a sight!

The wind giggles loudly, chasing those blooms,
They twirl and they spin, escaping their dooms.
One petal gets tangled, in a tree so spry,
But oh how it laughs, as it flutters on high!

"Catch me if you can!" the petals declare,
As the wind aims to toss them up in the air.
With each little flutter, there's mischief in play,
Who knew that flowers had games on display?

As twilight approaches, the breeze starts to tire,
Petals settle down, as if to conspire.
They exchange silly tales of their day so grand,
Who knew a gust could lend a helping hand?

Threads of Aromatic Memories

In the garden fair, scents twirl and twine,
A whiff of sweetness, the sun starts to shine.
Daisies remind us of childhood so vivid,
While lilies conspire, with mischief, they hid.

The fragrance of laughter, with each bloom's delight,
A spicy aroma ignites our wild night.
As the petals unravel, the air is alive,
With memories flickering, oh how they thrive!

A hint of nostalgia, the herb's gentle kiss,
In this fragrant playhouse, nothing's amiss.
Each flower tells stories, both funny and sweet,
As scents weave adventures with every heartbeat.

As twilight descends, the aromas conspire,
Laughter hangs thick, like smoke from a fire.
These threads of perfume bind us in cheer,
For every sweet scent brings loved ones near.

Marvel of Nature's Craftsmanship

Look at those petals, such crafty designs,
Nature's a genius, in so many lines.
Each flower a wonder, with quirks of all sorts,
They giggle with glee, in their floral court.

Some wear bright spikes, while others drape low,
A whimsical show, nature's own show.
With pincushions blooming, and trumpets so grand,
It's a wild gallery, best viewed unplanned!

Nature's a joker, with colors that clash,
Making fine art from a wild splash.
"Look at me!" they shout, in a colorful heap,
These talents of earth, oh, they're never cheap!

So here's to the blooms, those clowns of the land,
With their silly arrangements, oh isn't it grand?
A marvel indeed, crafted with flair,
In a world full of laughter, there's joy everywhere.

Journey of the Winged Messengers

In skies so bright, the birds do play,
Chasing sweet scents of a warm sunny day.
With flaps and hops, they sing so loud,
Each one thinks they're a superstar proud.

They flirt with bees, who buzz and tease,
As they dance among the swaying trees.
One bird tripped and fell with a flop,
Landed headfirst, oh, what a crop!

Through fields of green, their laughter flows,
Making jokes that only a sparrow knows.
With wings like capes, they soar with ease,
Turning every twig into a throne of peas.

When day is done, and they take a break,
Crowded on wires, they gossip and quake.
They plan for tomorrow, a wide airborne spree,
And laugh 'til they drop, as happy as can be.

Essence of the Tropics

In sunlit patches where laughter sways,
Fruits wear crowns in whimsical ways.
Each one's a trooper with a giggly grin,
Saying, "Pick me first, I'm juicy within!"

The pineapple shouts, "I'm a spiky delight!"
While coconuts roll like balls in a fight.
Bananas slip with a slippery cheer,
Yelling, "Peel us and toss away fear!"

All colors blend in a silly parade,
Mangoes blush as they try to evade.
"Catch me if you can!" the citrus sings,
While berries blush, hiding behind their flings.

Under the sun, they all dine together,
Creating a frenzy like a grand jester.
They share their secrets with giggles on cue,
In the essence of tropics, where happiness grew.

Whispers of Sweet Spring

The breeze whispers tales of bloom and play,
As flowers giggle in their own bright way.
Tulips tap dance, poking out their heads,
While daisies gossip about white flower beds.

The sun brings warmth, a tickle divine,
As blossoms cheer for their moment to shine.
"Look at me glow!" croaked a jolly tulip,
In a dress of pink, giving quite a flip!

With colors ablaze, they paint the town,
While bees do a jig, buzzing 'round with a frown.
"Why don't you dance?" a dandelion cried,
"Join in the fun, don't hide away inside!"

As petals shake loose, they twirl and spin,
Playing hopscotch with bugs on a whim.
In spring's funny realm, all worries shed,
Collecting bright laughs, like confetti, they spread!

Petals of Radiant Gold

In gardens of laughter, petals abound,
Golden delights dancing all around.
Sunflowers grin with a cheerful glare,
Swaying in rhythm, without a care.

With bees as the DJs, the tunes are spun,
Pollen parties where all have fun.
"Wanna join the jam?" the roses implore,
While tulips twirl, swishing all the more.

Petals drift down like a silly shower,
Making crowns for critters, oh what power!
"Wear it with pride!" chuckled a bold little bee,
"Together we bloom, oh what a spree!"

As day turns to dusk, twinkling starts peep,
The garden chuckles, secrets to keep.
In peaceful repose, they wink at the moon,
For laughter is gold, a sweet, radiant tune.

Sweet Petals in the Sun

In the garden, quite a sight,
Colorful blooms play with the light.
A bee zooms by, with a bumble and dance,
"Hey there, flower! Care for a chance?"

Petals giggle, swaying in glee,
Fluttering softly, full of esprit.
A grasshopper's joke, a caterpillar's laugh,
"Who ordered the sunshine? Oh, what a gaffe!"

Rustling leaves, a tickle in the air,
"Must we all share? Just a touch of flair!"
The sun grins down, as if in on the fun,
"Hey little blooms, let's play on the run!"

With buddies around, life's a bright spree,
Colors and laughter, what a jubilee!
In this floral party, no worries descend,
Just petal-shaped giggles that never quite end.

Nectar's Whispers

In a sunny nook, where laughter does flow,
Tiny creatures come, all dressed up to show.
A clever old bee sings a tune to his friend,
"Got nectar as sweet as a candy you send!"

Butterflies linger, with wings made for style,
They flit and they flutter, oh, what a while!
"Did you see that poodle?" one whispers in glee,
"It bounced down the path—an absolute spree!"

And as flowers chuckle, secrets unfold,
"Let's dance with the breeze, watch the day turn gold!"
With giggles and sways, the garden's alive,
Every petal joins in, it's a bustling hive.

"What's the flavor today?" a squirrel asks with flair,
"Let's mix it with laughter, lighten up the air!"
In this buzz of joy, humor finds its place,
With nectar so rich, we'll float in good grace.

Blossoms of Summer's Embrace

Under skies of azure, blooms start to tease,
With colors so vibrant, dancing in the breeze.
A chubby old toad croaks, "What's buzzing so loud?
Is it just me, or did that flower just bow?"

Petals prance lightly, a colorful choir,
"Let's twirl with joy, and play on the wire!"
With a wink and a nod, daisies make way,
"Come join the laugh fest, we'll frolic all day!"

Sipping sunlight, honey-like dreams,
Fluttering softly, they share silly schemes.
"A raindrop just fell! Did you hear the big splat?
Let's fashion a hat, oh, how 'bout that?"

Embraced by warm summer, the garden's aglow,
Tickled by laughter, it's all on show.
A trumpet of petals, a jolly serenade,
In nature's grand comedy, fun's never delayed!

Fruitful Dreams Beneath the Leaves

Beneath leafy arches, where the sunshine spills,
Witty little critters indulge in their thrills.
"Did you see that squirrel? He just took a dive!
Thought he could fly but just landed in jive!"

With whispers and chuckles, the night owl hoots,
"Let's gather together in our fruity suits!"
A playful old raccoon, sparks joy with a smirk,
"Join the fruit party! Let's dance and go berserk!"

The vines sway gently, smiling all around,
"Feeling fruity today? Let's make merry sounds!"
In the shade, where laughter and mischief unite,
Every flick of a leaf glimmers with delight.

"Who knew leaves could giggle and twinkle so bright?
Our underworld ballet is quite the sheer sight!"
As fun fills the air, beneath branches we lay,
In dreams soaked with laughter, we greet the new day.

Blossoms Beneath the Canopy

Under the green, where shadows play,
A dance of petals, bright as the day.
They flutter like butterflies, oh what a sight,
Some whisper secrets, while others take flight.

A squirrel's bold leap, what a clumsy fall,
Leaves rustle with laughter, a vibrant call.
The fruits roll their eyes, they're quite the scene,
Wishing for sunshine, they dream of routine.

In this leafy kingdom, giggles arise,
As bees with their buzz come under disguise.
A petal parade, oh what a fuss,
Waving red flags, they complain and discuss.

So here in the shade, let joy be our theme,
For life is a circus, or so it would seem.
With blossoms above, we'll dance and we'll prance,
In the cool of the shade, let's take a chance!

A Dance of Sunlit Petals

In the morning light, they sway with glee,
Bouncing along, as happy as can be.
With each little breeze, they rustle and giggle,
Playing hide and seek, oh what a wiggle!

A bee with a bow tie, so dapper, so sweet,
Tries to join in on the tropical beat.
The petals just chuckle, they prance in delight,
While the sun shines down with all of its light.

There's a leaf with a laugh, a curious scene,
Telling the blossoms, "You should join the routine!"
Up and around, they twirl and they spin,
"Let's dance 'til the day ends, let good times begin!"

With petals a-laughing, we join in their play,
For life is much brighter when joy leads the way.
So clap your hands softly, let's keep up the cheer,
For when petals are dancing, there's nothing to fear!

Nectar-kissed Dreams

In a world of sweet dreams, where laughter is gold,
A nectar-filled tale of beauty unfolds.
Sticky and sunny, the fruit sings its song,
Begging me temptingly to join in along.

A cheeky little monkey swings by with a grin,
Sniffing the sweetness, he's ready to win.
If only the blossoms could see his bright face,
They'd giggle and dance in a fruit-loving race.

Beneath leafy arches, all flavors conspire,
To craft all the stories that dreams can aspire.
With each buzzing laugh, the day feels so fine,
It's a carnival of joy where the sun always shines!

Just close your eyes and take in the air,
With nectar-laden wishes, let go of your care.
In this whimsical world, let your laughter flow,
For in dreams made of nectar, our hearts surely glow!

Fragrance of the Tropics

Oh, the tangy aroma that dances so free,
Filling the air like a sweet symphony.
The sun peeks through branches, a cheeky surprise,
Tickling the petals that giggle and rise.

A troupe of small critters is planning a feast,
With juicy delights, they'll never be ceased.
"Let's hop on a breeze, let's have some fun!"
The fruits all reply, "We're not done, we've just begun!"

So gather 'round closely, let good times commence,
With chatter and laughter, there's no need for pretense.
The scent of the tropics, a laugh in the sky,
Reminds us that joy is the reason to fly.

With petals all twirling, our spirits so high,
In this fragrant fiesta, together we'll sigh.
For the mood of the day is as light as a breeze,
In the tropics' embrace, we'll dance with such ease!

www.ingramcontent.com/pod-product-compliance
Lightning Source LLC
Chambersburg PA
CBHW060144230426
43661CB00003B/557